This book says a lot of things I'd like you to hold close to your heart forever.

But most of all, I want it to remind you, in all the days to come...

You have your whole life ahead of you, and I want it to be a wonderful one.

— Douglas Pagels

Happy 16th Birthday!!
We love you lots,
Your godparents ~
Uncle Burt & Aunt Cheryl

Required Reading for All Teenagers

(Or at least one who is very important to me!)

Updated Edition

Written and Edited by
Douglas Pagels

Featuring illustrations by
Kristin Sheldon

Blue Mountain Press™
Boulder, Colorado

Copyright © 2005, 2011 by Blue Mountain Arts, Inc.

Illustrations by Kristin Sheldon. Copyright © 2005, 2011 by Kristin Sheldon. Used by permission.

Library of Congress Control Number: 2010914667
ISBN: 978-1-59842-599-4

♔ and Blue Mountain Press are registered in U.S. Patent and Trademark Office.
Certain trademarks are used under license.

Acknowledgments appear on page 92.

Printed in China.
Second printing of this edition: 2012

♻ This book is printed on recycled paper.

This book is printed on paper that has been specially produced to be acid free (neutral pH) and contains no groundwood or unbleached pulp. It conforms with the requirements of the American National Standards Institute, Inc., so as to ensure that this book will last and be enjoyed by future generations.

Blue Mountain Arts, Inc.
P.O. Box 4549, Boulder, Colorado 80306

Contents

(Authors listed in order of first appearance)

We're growing and we're going through a lot of things in our lives.

❖ Selena Gomez

I am in a transitional period in a lot of different ways. I am changing and making lots of decisions about my future. It's a very exciting and slightly scary time.

— Emma Watson

It is wonderful to be a teenager, but it's scary, too. You're growing up, making more of your own choices, and finding out who you are. You've got to start thinking about some serious stuff....

I think that it's safe to say that you're never going to go through another seven years in your life that are as confusing or as exciting as adolescence. This is *the* period in your life specifically designed for you to dream, to plan, to think, and to determine who it is you want to be from this time forward.

— Joni Arredia

Just remember from one who's been there, give it time and believe in yourself. Listen to good advice from those who care about you.

— Niki Taylor

I'll Always Be Here for You

I want you to promise me that you'll remember this...

No one's happiness is more important to me than yours is.

There are days when my whole world revolves around you.
There are times when I know things are going well for you,
and when that happens, it seems like I smile myself to sleep.

There are moments when life has been unfair to you, and my
heart just breaks... knowing what you're going through.

Some people might say that it's just my job... to want to help
out. But as far as I'm concerned, it's the most important job
in the world... and I wouldn't trade it for anything. I will be
here to love you, to listen to you, to support every hope and
dream I can.

So, if there is ever anything (and I really mean anything) you
need to talk over or work out... or if there's something I can
do, I want you to know you can turn to me.

I'll always be here for you.

— Douglas Pagels

Know that you are loved by the people who matter forever. Keep gazing out your window every night into the universe, and remind yourself there is something greater than all of us. Focus on and reach for the stars and, I promise you, you'll be one too.
— Mýa Harrison

One of the great things about being young is that your future is wide open.
— Carol Weston

You are capable of more than you know. Choose a goal that seems right for you and strive to be the best, however hard the path. Aim high... Persist! The world needs all you can give.
— Edward O. Wilson

Give from your heart, and each day will be a blessing.

— Jada Pinkett Smith

Make each day, each stage in your life, your best. This isn't something that just happens if you're lucky. You make this contentment happen. You make the choices. Your life will be what you make it.

And your happiness comes from within you, not from the money you make, the trips you take, or the things you own.

— Faith Stewart

It's your choice. Always look for the hidden blessings, even in your darkest moments; I promise they are there. You cannot control many things that will happen to you, but you can control how you see them.

Choose to see them in a way that lifts you up, not brings you down.

— Sara Blakely

Every day I wake up and count my blessings.

❖ Justin Bieber

You Hold the Key

I've got something to say to you, and I hope you will listen with an open heart. Don't be so worried about what everybody else thinks of you, and don't think your happiness depends on someone else. I want you to just trust yourself. Trust that if you take care of yourself on the inside, follow your instincts, and let yourself evolve naturally, your potential for happiness will be so much greater.

— Trisha Yearwood

This was the turning point for me. I was forced to believe in myself and not in what others thought of me. It was one of the hardest lessons I've ever gone through, and it changed my life forever.

— Alicia Keys

Has anyone told you lately... what a wonderful person you are?

I hope so! I hope you've been told dozens of times... because you are just amazing. And in case you haven't heard those words in a while, I want you to hear them now. You deserve to know that...

It takes someone special to do what you do. It takes someone rare and remarkable to make the lives of everyone around them so much nicer. It takes someone everyone can be proud of... a youthful soul who is learning and growing and going toward the horizons that lie ahead. It takes someone who is living proof of how precious a person can be.

It takes someone... just like you.

— Douglas Pagels

Whatever your goal, I hope you discover — just like I did... that success isn't only about the goal you choose. It's about the experience, the effort, and the journey.

❖ Annika Sorenstam

Dreams are your destination.... Without dreams, life happens to you. With dreams, you make life happen.

You need big dreams, little dreams, and in-between dreams. Dreams for your teen years, and dreams beyond. You should spend time now thinking about your dreams. Once you know what they are, you need to learn how to live them, and never give them up.

— Joni Arredia

You have everything you need inside of you already. You don't have to see the whole journey laid out in front of you so you can "plan" for it. Honor the magic; be present for the adventure. Just trust that if you get from A to B, the next step C (or whatever letter you jump to!) will reveal itself. Keep the dreamer alive. It's who you really are.

— Aimee Mullins

To Achieve Your Dreams, Remember Your ABCS

Avoid negative sources, people, places, things, and habits.

Believe in yourself.

Consider things from every angle.

Don't give up and don't give in.

Enjoy life today.

Family and friends are hidden treasures.

Give more than you planned to.

Hang on to your dreams.

Ignore those who try to discourage you.

Just do it.

Keep trying, no matter how hard it seems.

Love yourself first and foremost.

Make room somewhere for letting others in.

Never lie, cheat, or steal; always strike a fair deal.

Open your heart, and your eyes will see things as they really are.

Practice makes perfect.

Quitters never win and winners never quit.

Read, study, and learn about everything important in the world.

Stop procrastinating.

Take control of your own destiny.

Understand yourself in order to better understand others.

Visualize it with a picture-perfect mind.

Want it more than anything.

Xcelerate your efforts.

You are unique... nothing can replace you.

Zero in on your target and go for it!

— Author Unknown

"Never, Never, Never Give Up"
(Taylor Swift's Motto)

Basically, all the record companies went, "Ah, how cute. She's just a little kid." They also said, "Give up your dreams. Go home and come back when you're 18." I chose not to hear that. I wasn't prepared to accept that I wasn't a relevant artist until I was 18, and so I just kept coming back.

— Taylor Swift

Learn to make a way out of no way. Believe you can make a difference and then do it.... Never, *never* give up. Remember the saying that "there is not enough darkness in the world to snuff out the light of even one small candle." So let your light shine.

— Marian Wright Edelman

Dreams come a size
too big so that we can
grow into them.

❖ Josie Bisset

Words to Help You Be Strong Along the Path of Life

I can barely begin to tell you of all my wishes for you ✦ There are so many of them, and I want them all to come true ✦ I want you to use your heart as a compass as you grow and find your way in the world, but I want you to always have an appreciation for the direction of home ✦ I want you to have self-esteem and self-confidence and to be self-sufficient, but also to know that you will never be alone ✦ I want you to be safe and smart and cautious ✦ I want you to be wise beyond your years ✦ I don't want you to grow up too fast ✦ I want you to come to me with your fears ✦ I want the people who share your days to realize that they are in the presence of a very special someone ✦ You are a wonderful, rare person with no comparison ✦

I want you to know that opportunities will come, and you'll have many goals to achieve ♦ The more that obstacles get in the way of your dreams, the more you'll need to believe ♦ Get your feet wet with new experiences, but be sure you never get in over your head ♦ I want you to realize how capable you are and that your possibilities are unlimited ♦ I hope you never lose your childlike wonder, your delight and appreciation in interesting things ♦ I know you'll keep responding in a positive way to the challenges life always brings ♦ I want you to set the stage for living in a way that reflects good choices and a great attitude ♦ I want you to honor... the wonder of you ♦

— Douglas Pagels

"How does one become a butterfly?" she asked pensively.

"You must want to fly so much that you are willing to give up being a caterpillar."

❖ Trina Paulus

I want you to enjoy your life without the burdens that come with growing up too soon. I want you to have an opportunity to daydream about what you want to be when you grow up. I want you to be carefree, even as you learn how to gradually handle responsibility. I want to protect you even as I encourage you to mature, to grow, to fly.

You cannot expect to grow up overnight. We grow and mature in stages. Can you remember what you were like when you were six years old? Ten years old? You were very different then than you are now, right? Well, you will be different at fourteen, sixteen, eighteen, and twenty-one. You shouldn't treat life like you do a [movie] when you hit what you feel is a dull part; you shouldn't try to fast-forward yourself....

Just as you've had only one childhood, you will have only one go-round as an adolescent. Enjoy just being a teenager now!

— Joyce A. Ladner

I believe that all of us truly need teaching on this subject of how to enjoy where we are on the way to where we are going.

— Joyce Meyer

Life is a succession of lessons which must be lived to be understood.

— Ralph Waldo Emerson

Whatever good you put out in the universe [will] come back, and whatever bad you put out [will] come back as well.

— Oprah Winfrey

It's Pretty Much Up to You!

Decisions are incredibly important things! Good decisions will come back to bless you. Bad decisions can come back to haunt you.

That's why it's so important that you take the time to choose wisely. Choose to do the things that reflect well... on your ability, your integrity, your spirit, your health, your tomorrows, your smiles, your dreams, and yourself.

You are such a wonder. You're the only one in the universe exactly like you! I want you to take care of that rare and remarkable soul. I want you to know that there is someone who will thank you for doing the things you do now with foresight and wisdom and respect.

It's the person you will someday be. You have a chance to make that person so thankful and so proud. All you have to do is remember one of the lessons I learned when I made a similar journey. It's pretty simple, really; just these eight words:

Each time you're given the chance...
choose wisely.
— Douglas Pagels

As simple as it sounds, we all must try to be the best person we can: by making the best choices, by making the most of the talents we've been given.

— Mary Lou Retton

I'm still in the process of discovering who I am, but... I'm much happier now than I have been in years. It's still hard to separate my thoughts from my feelings, but at least I know there is a difference. I'm coming to realize that I do have a lot of choices, and that good choices have good consequences and that bad choices have bad consequences.

— Lucy Smith (age 16)

A person of integrity lurks somewhere inside each of us: a person we feel we can trust to do right, to play by the rules, to keep commitments.

— Stephen L. Carter

My daily mission is to... become a better decision maker.

❖ Brandi Chastain

27

In junior high, I was surrounded by classmates who were making bad decisions, and it wasn't appealing to me at all. I started hanging out with an older group. I wanted to be accepted, but since they were into the party scene, I felt more pressure than I did in my other peer group....

I was doing things I never thought I would, and I just felt dumb and gross. It was a learning experience I came out of saying, "I know I don't want to do that. I know I don't want to go there again." I was trying too hard to fit in. I wasn't being genuine with myself.

When it comes to dealing with peer pressure, my philosophy is that I have to make my decisions beforehand about what I will and won't do. We can set our standards ahead of time. Then, when we're faced with a tough choice, there won't be any question about how to answer, and we won't get caught in the moment!

— Stacie Orrico

Let's face it. Peer pressure is tough and real, and sometimes you just can't help but give in. We are all only human, and it is a natural process to go through, especially in high school and college. Peer pressure is a really hard thing to avoid and an even harder thing to be around. Listen to your gut feelings in those situations. You may feel like a loser for not trying something in the moment, but think about the aftermath of the situation and the potential negative consequences. Take one moment before you take a drink or hit of something and really consider the possibilities if you get caught, or worse, hurt someone else or yourself. In the end, you will be in a much better place for choosing not to participate. And remember, above all, if you are with friends who didn't say no, don't get into the car with them. Call your parents or catch a ride with someone else.

— Katherine Schwarzenegger

Never do something to make
people like you if it's going
to end up making you
like yourself less.

❖ Nancy Holyoke

To make people happy, I would try to accommodate everyone's desires even if it meant it would make me miserable. So when I would hit a bump in the road, I would often cave in to other people's wishes or demands because I wanted to please them....

The result is people take advantage of you, you lose self-respect, and in the end, you end up unhappy.

— Scott Hamilton

If you know ahead of time what things you will and won't do, you will feel much more confident when you are in a decision-making situation. You can set boundaries concerning how you will allow people to treat you and how much you are willing to give in a friendship or romantic relationship, and the kinds of risks you are willing to take in general.

Setting boundaries and sticking to them is a challenge. But each time you do it and you experience how good it feels, it becomes easier. Remember: Your boundaries are your own. If you are firm in your convictions, other people's opinions cannot shake them. There might be those who try to get you to do things that feel wrong to you. But remember, the people who really love you and have your best interests at heart will respect your limits.

— Kimberly Kirberger

I think if you don't love yourself first,
no one else will love you.

— Selena Gomez

When you remember what you love, you will remember who
you are. If you remember who you are, you can do anything.

— Cathy Guisewite

The best advice I have ever received was to love and believe
in myself and my abilities, and to be proud of who I was...
If you don't love yourself, then you cannot expect others to
love you. Also, there are some people in the world who will
insult you, or put you down, and try to convince you that
something is wrong with you so that they can feel a sense
of power, and if you don't believe in yourself you'll start to
believe them.

— Anonymous (age 16)

Stand Up for What You Believe!

Once you know what is right and wrong, you must stand up for your beliefs. When someone is doing the wrong thing, it is time to speak out. This world needs more people with the courage to act on their beliefs. Don't be afraid to speak against injustice. Even if you are picked on for taking a stand and for having high ideals, you must persevere.

— Rebecca Lobo

A lot of people are looking at you and judging you and talking about you... That's difficult to deal with, just because of the weird things they say about you.

You just have to realize they are people who don't know you. But you know who you are, and your friends know who you are. If you're not able to block it out, you would go crazy.

— Emma Roberts

I have found that being active in your school can keep you somewhat sane. True, it can get stressful with the tests, the homework, and the few difficult teachers who are "out to get you," but as long as you find something that is intriguing, high school won't seem so stressful, and it won't seem like forever. My crazy life of running about has shown me that high school is not one of the worst things that can happen to you, but really one of the best.

— Amanda (age 16)

Of everything that you go through in high school, you must have one thing that will keep you sane. You gotta have something to look forward to, at least one thing during your not-so-long stay at high school. Some teacher you like the most, some class you absolutely enjoy, some performance for the year that your school does, whatever floats your boat.

— Michael (age 18)

Life is a river,
and we all have to find
a boat that floats.

❖ Thad Carhart

School exposes you to so much: Shakespeare's plays, Einstein's calculations, Picasso's paintings. Sooner or later, while you're writing a program in computer class, conducting a fruit-fly experiment in biology, racing around the track, singing in the chorus, or putting a pot in the kiln, you'll feel filled with energy and enthusiasm. You'll begin to figure out what you like to do, what you're best at, what fields of study to pursue, or what career to start aiming for. That's an exciting discovery. You'll also learn what you're not good at and not interested in, which helps in planning your future, too.

Whether you're in junior high or high school, dabble with electives, sports, and "extracurrics." Balance your schedule without overloading it. The more you learn, the more things you'll enjoy and the more choices you'll have. If you can't type or aren't computer literate, you're limiting your marketable skills.

If you don't like reading or theater or sculpture, you have fewer ways to enjoy yourself than someone who does. Do you know the basics of auto mechanics? You're one up on the person who panics whenever her car sputters.

You'll never regret having that education edge. School teaches you to think, to analyze, to solve problems, and to work with discipline. Not all your teachers are brilliant and amiable, but not all your future employers will be, either. Not every assignment is scintillating and important, but in the Real World, there are dirty dishes to wash and boring bills to pay no matter how exhilarating your profession is. Besides, the best ticket out of a boring school is to do well there.

Your education, in and out of school, is for you — so you'll be able to lead your life instead of being led by it.

— Carol Weston

I feel like there are a lot of different things that can educate you in life.

❖ Taylor Swift

Hitting the Books

Serena and I believe there's nothing more important in life than getting a good education. We want you to become so determined to learn that you don't allow anyone or anything to come between you and your schoolwork....

The people and conditions in your life change from day to day. But the things you learn will always stay with you. Knowledge is the one thing that no one can take away from you — ever, no matter what. This is really important for you to understand.... The more you learn, the better your future will be and the more choices you'll have.

— Venus Williams

I would suggest getting involved in activities your school provides or obtaining a job to set yourself apart from others, and to realize early on that you do have a wonderful future ahead of you.

— Shali (age 17)

If you knew you were going to be stranded on a deserted island for four years, you would immediately start thinking about what you would need to survive during those four years. Well, high school can be very much like that deserted island. What will you need to get through these four years?

High school is a time when a sense of belonging, support, and being part of something can really help students succeed academically, stay out of trouble, and ease some of the feelings of loneliness and not fitting in. Whether you're drawn to the football team, the band, the chess club or stage crew, or an internship, community service, or part-time job, the important thing is to have *something*.

— Jane Bluestein and Eric Katz

There is some place where your specialties can shine. Somewhere that difference can be expressed. It's up to you to find it, and you can.
— David Viscott

You don't get to pick who you are in this life, but you can decide what you become.
— Jodee Blanco

My message to teens... is to look for your own strengths.
— Brooke Shields

To be the best at anything, you have to be strong. You have to be willing to overcome all the obstacles that get in your way, and you have to make sacrifices.

— Celine Dion

Stay Strong!

A strong body means your muscles are toned, you have endurance and flexibility, and you have enough energy for work and play.

A strong mind means you have a positive attitude, can make healthy decisions, are clearheaded and open to challenges, and are willing to think for yourself.

A strong spirit means you have faith in yourself, are in tune with your inner voice, and can bounce back when things don't go your way.

— Tina Schwager, PTA, ATC and Michele Schuerger

Promise me you'll always remember: you're braver than you believe, and stronger than you seem, and smarter than you think.

❖ Christopher Robin to Winnie-the-Pooh

Checking Out That Person in the Mirror

You are something — and someone — very special. You really are. No one else in this entire world is exactly like you, and there are so many incredible things about you.

You're a one-of-a-kind treasure, uniquely here in this space and time. You are here to shine in your own wonderful way, sharing your smile in the best way you can, and remembering all the while that a little light somewhere makes a brighter light everywhere. You can — and you do — make a wonderful contribution to this world.

You have qualities within you that many people would love to have, and those who really and truly know you... are so glad that they do. You have a big heart and a good and sensitive soul. You are gifted with thoughts and ways of seeing things that only special people know. You know that life doesn't always play by the rules, but that in the long run, everything will work out.

You understand that you and your actions are capable of turning anything around — and that joys once lost can always be found. There is a resolve and an inner reserve of strength in you that few ever get to see. You have so many treasures within — those you're only beginning to discover, and all the ones you're already aware of.

Never forget what a treasure you are. That special person in the mirror may not always get to hear all the compliments you so sweetly deserve, but

    you are so worthy of
        such an abundance
            ...of friendship, joy, and love.

— Douglas Pagels

I am aware that I am less than some people would prefer me to be, but most people are unaware that I am so much more than what they see.

❖ Douglas Pagels

Learning to love yourself has to begin with the realization that sometimes you don't. Try not to judge yourself or get frustrated when you're dealing with difficult thoughts or emotions. Instead, remember that you are getting to know yourself in a deeper, more meaningful way.

— Kimberly Kirberger

Do I love my body? It's almost unrealistic to say you love your body because most of us have parts of our bodies we don't love and never will. I still have some baggage. I think it's important to accept that we are who we are, but it's our responsibility to give ourselves the best shot at learning how to be comfortable with our body — eating properly, getting movement, not smoking....

Remember, your best friend and worst enemy is the person you see in the mirror.

— Leslie Goldman

The most important thing in life is not what happens to you but your attitude toward what happens to you.

— Richard Heyman

Every day of your life, something or someone is going to throw something at you that will challenge your ability to rise above negativity... But you have to remember in these trying moments that it isn't the events in your life that define you; it's how you deal with them.

Every time I was thrown a curve, I had to find a way to deal with it. I don't know how I was able to do it sometimes. I just know that each time I was faced with something, I would try to find the positive side.

— Scott Hamilton

I've always believed that you can think positive just as well as you can think negative.

— Sugar Ray Robinson

People who have a strong positive sense of themselves generally lead much happier lives. They rarely suffer from eating disorders, are less likely to become alcohol- or drug-dependent, are able to handle stress well, and get along with other people. If there are stresses, they believe they can deal with them (or will forgive themselves if they can't). If their bodies aren't "perfect," they can accept that, and a negative comment doesn't mean the end of the world.

— Nancy Rubin

When I became a teenager, I experienced times when I felt insecure about my looks. I wished that my face were more attractive... and wished that I were slimmer....

During those years there were many times I wished that I could mix and match body parts with someone else.... Over time, my physical features all caught up with one another and everything balanced out. As that happened, I started to come into my own and grow comfortable in my skin. At some point it just dawned on me that this is the body God gave me and I love and appreciate it no matter what.

— Serena Williams

If you find you have a problem with eating or have a friend who does, get help. If you can't talk to your mother about it, go to your best friend, a teacher, a coach, a youth-group leader, or anyone that you trust.... When you find that you would rather be skinny than healthy, you have a problem.

— Amanda Ford

I have been vigilant to remember what does and doesn't matter in life.

❖ Mary Steenburgen

I think actress Kate Winslet... has one of the best attitudes in Hollywood when it comes to fitness.

"I am who I am," she says. "I'm healthy. I swim a mile every day. I'll never be a stick insect, and I wouldn't want to be either, because it seems to me that a lot of people who are very thin are just really unhappy.

"I had a time in my life when I was about nineteen and I was very thin, and I wasn't eating. I was anorexic for about six months, and I was so unhappy....

"I feel for those people [anorexics] because they're being screwed up by what is said to be beautiful and successful these days, thin and pretty, and it's just 'a crock.'

"Because of the person I am, I won't be knocked down — ever. They can do what they like," she says. "They can say I'm fat, I'm thin, I'm whatever, and I'll never stop. I just won't. I've got too much to do. I've too much to be happy about."

— Kathy Kaehler

While body type is something you're born with and can't necessarily change, you can change your eating habits and up your level of physical activity.... Never forget that you can firm, tone, define, and enhance what you already have through fitness. Fitness is always a positive way of dealing with everything. It also provides a great release from the mental and emotional frustrations that come with being a teen.

— Kathy Kaehler

I want you to know that your hormones are much stronger than you think, and they are responsible for a lot of what you're feeling. Of course what you are feeling is still real, but it is terribly exaggerated by natural chemical changes in your body.

— Magali Amadei

Being a teenager is hard for everyone. My advice? Have compassion (especially for yourself) and stick together. You're all in the same hormonal boat.

❖ Phoebe Cates

If I could say anything to teenage girls it would be, "You're not alone."

— Jessica Alba

I would like to tell *both* sexes to relax! Everybody seems so uptight and so many people lose themselves trying to impress others, when honesty and openness would make things go over so much more easily. I wish people would stop trying to be what they're not, accept what they are, and work from there. The smallest lie, to oneself or to others, can cause the deepest and cruelest pain. In general, I think a deeper self-awareness and realization would make life a lot easier; and openness, honesty, and friendship would make for a smoother running "world in one peace" which can cope with itself for the benefit of everyone and everything.

— Anonymous (age 16)

Relax – Things Will Get Better (Much, Much Better)

As a result of my physical appearance, I was subjected to all of the embarrassment and ridicule childhood had to offer. I was called names, tripped in the hallways, and excluded from activities. I went out of my way to avoid [those] who already seemed to have adjusted to the physical changes of their bodies and shifting social climate of early adolescence. Their confidence only made me feel more unattractive and unhappy....

I constantly held myself up to others, comparing myself to what I considered perfect standards, and was never happy with what I saw. I sacrificed all of my own tastes and preferences, and in the process lost all sense of my own individuality.

During my first day of classes at college, I was hit with a reality that would change everything. Settling into my first class, I looked all around me and saw an amazing collection of different kinds of people. They were dressed in different ways and came from many different places. It occurred to me that we were each there to learn and to prepare for our future — not to compete for social status and not to struggle for acceptance. I felt as though a blindfold had been untied from my eyes, and I saw that maintaining a certain image and hiding my own personality here was not only unnecessary but also an injustice to myself....

I suddenly understood that although people are often judged on their looks, labeled as one thing or another, and placed into categories, they have a choice in whether or not they allow themselves to be defined by others. All through school, I had accepted my label and my category as the truth. I now recognized that no one had the power to define who I was but *me* — and there was much more to who I was besides my physical appearance.

— Kelly Garnett

I was always looking outside myself for strength and confidence, but it comes from within. It was there all the time.

— Anna Freud

I was an eighteen-year-old kid with creativity, talent, and potential. I was also an eighteen-year-old kid who was insecure, highly self-critical, and prone to dark moods of doubt and depression....

The thing I have had to work on most diligently is correcting these negative tendencies because if they go unchecked they can run rampant. I have had to work hard and stay constantly focused — why am I so hard on myself... why do I doubt so often... why am I sad?...

Through the years, I have regained myself. I have also learned to access that miraculous center I lived in so instinctively as a child. It has never been lost. It was only buried. My light wasn't damaged or broken. It was wrapped in layers of doubt and insecurity. Somehow, just knowing that seemed to help a lot. Now it's just a question of remembering what's inside me and acting on it, day by day.

— Jewel

It's a noisy world and the answer inside you sometimes has trouble being heard. But take the time to quietly listen and you'll never go wrong.

❖ Piper Perabo

Do the Right Thing!

There are a lot of temptations in the world. We make many choices every day, some of which are very difficult. When making a decision, you must feel good about yourself and confident that you are doing the right thing. If you don't feel comfortable making a certain decision, if your gut tells you something isn't right, then it probably isn't.

— Rebecca Lobo

I'm hoping you don't smoke or drink or do drugs.... The patterns you set now may be yours for keeps. You owe it to yourself to find out what you're getting into. You owe it to yourself to take care of your body.

— Carol Weston

I don't like to abuse alcohol — anything you abuse will abuse you back.

— Bono

I don't need to tell you how stupid and dangerous drugs are. (Do I?) Just in case you're wondering, besides robbing you of your self-esteem and a bright future, these illegal substances can be extremely rough on you inside and out.

— Bobbi Brown

I will tell you that I don't want you to drink or do drugs for the following reasons. When you're drunk or high, it's harder to make the responsible choices that can keep you safe. The facts are that bad things happen to really smart people when they drink and use drugs. I'm worried that someone will take advantage of you when you're drunk or high. I'm also really worried about you getting into a car with someone who's drunk or high. But I can't control what you do. When you're away from me, I've got to hope that you'll make choices that will keep you safe and out of trouble.

— Rosalind Wiseman

Make choices that keep the peace and make you feel proud of how you represent yourself.

❖ Venus Williams

I have lost a lot of friends... they became addicted to various substances. They could never feel how far was too far. They thought that they could handle anything, stay in control of the substances that were making them feel invincible, that were egging them on to cross any boundary....

We always have an "it won't happen to me" attitude when we see other people making mistakes. Don't be fooled. It can happen to you — if you aren't careful, if you don't know who you are — anything can happen.

— Queen Latifah

Twenty-Four Things to Always Remember... and One Thing to Never Forget

Your presence is a present to the world.
You're unique and one of a kind.
Your life can be what you want it to be.
Take the days just one at a time.

Count your blessings, not your troubles.
You'll make it through whatever comes along.
Within you are so many answers.
Understand, have courage, be strong.

Don't put limits on yourself.
So many dreams are waiting to be realized.
Decisions are too important to leave to chance.
Reach for your peak, your goal, your prize.

Nothing wastes more energy than worrying.
The longer one carries a problem,
	the heavier it gets.
Don't take things too seriously.
Live a life of serenity, not a life of regrets.

Remember that a little love goes a long way.
Remember that a lot... goes forever.
Remember that friendship is a wise investment.
Life's treasures are people... together.

Realize that it's never too late.
Do ordinary things in an extraordinary way.
Have health and hope and happiness.
Take the time to wish upon a star.

And don't ever forget...
	for even a day... how very special you are.

— Douglas Pagels

Stand for Something
or You'll Fall for Anything

I wanted everybody to love *me* so badly that for years I let other people's plans and priorities run my life. I allowed others to take from me without giving back, to goad or guilt me into solving their problems, to use me for their own ends, all because I was scared of losing their love and approval....

People who *really* love you don't put conditions on their feelings. They don't say, "I'll love you as long as you do what I want you to." Or, "I'll love you on the condition you continue to please me." They say, "I love you" — period, end of sentence.

Since I reached this understanding, it's impossible to overstate how different my life is. How much richer and fuller and *easier*. While I'm not insensitive to the needs and wants of others, I have learned how crucial it is to honor my own.

— Patti LaBelle

Character is made by
what you stand for;
reputation by
what you fall for.

❖ Robert Quillen

Don't Post That Picture

In this day and age, just about everyone is on social networking sites, sharing more about their private lives than ever before. Sharing, connecting, and communicating on the Internet are like a lot of things. There's a really good side... and there's a really bad side. The side that can suddenly change everything for the worse can rear its ugly head if you don't understand the consequences of posting personal pictures and information. The rule of thumb should be this: if you wouldn't want your parents, teachers, or grandparents to see it or read it, don't post it.

You may think you're only sharing that embarrassing story with your friends, but you're not. And if you have the impression that the cell phone picture you're thinking of sending to just one special person will stop there, you're being too naive... and gambling with way too much. When a regrettable picture winds up online, it can be there forever... for anyone in the world to see. It can shadow you throughout your entire life. It can affect future plans, schools, jobs, and relationships. That's a sad truth and a sorry situation. But there is a solution to the problem: just don't do it to begin with. It's as easy, as rewarding, and as reassuring as that.

— Douglas Pagels

People... can constantly put you in an uncomfortable and vulnerable position. I learned this the hard way. By the time I found the courage to voice my feelings, a magazine was already on the newsstands, on *every* corner, with a photograph that embarrassed me, and I had to live with it. There was nothing I could do about it. It was devastating to me because it presented me in a light that I didn't want to stand in and worse, I hadn't felt comfortable with the photo shoot all along. I just didn't know how to say no to them because I was inexperienced. So I doubted myself, but in my gut I knew the whole time that it wasn't right.

Long after, in my mind, I tried to find reasons to justify it, but the only justification I could come up with was that this was something that showed me how strong I would have to be to stand up for what I believe to be true, no matter what some fool thinks. That fool doesn't have to sleep with my conscience every night.

— Alicia Keys

If you ignore what you
know to be the difference
between right and wrong,
you'll pay a huge price.
And I'm not just talking
about losing sleep.

❖ Maria Shriver

The Internet is a wonderful resource when used responsibly, but it can put kids at risk since it doesn't discriminate when it comes to communication and the exchange of information between honest, reliable people and organizations, and those who seek to exploit the young, innocent, and gullible.... Anyone can have a website, anyone can say anything he wants, anyone can offer things for sale, anyone can pretend to be someone or something he is not.

— Richard Heyman

[My parents] found ways to separate me from electricity for full days and weeks....

Their relentless efforts were unwelcome at the time, but they made it impossible for me to ignore the fact that there was a very big world out there — with actual people I could see and touch! This probably kept me safely away from the edge that some guys go over when electronic socializing takes the place of interacting with real people almost entirely....

No matter how advanced or amazing computers, TV shows, and movies get, they will never be able to replace real life.

— Greg Fuller

Thirteen Things I Don't Want You to Do

Don't ~ stress out about things you have no control over. Sometimes what is... just is.

Don't ~ waste your days in emotional disarray over a negative situation that you *can* be in control of. (Remember, you always have *at least* three options: move on; stay where you are and just deal with it; or turn a negative situation into a positive one.)

Don't ~ try to fit in with the "right" crowd when it feels too forced. The best friendships are the ones that are natural and easy and comfortable and kind. Find one of those.

Don't ~ be a part of prejudice against anyone. Be colorblind, and be open-minded to the millions who have diverse beliefs and varying backgrounds.

Don't ~ worry about your future. It will unfold slowly enough and give you plenty of time to help you decide... all the wheres and whens and whys.

Don't ~ feel like you have to put up with people who are rude or obnoxious. Always take the higher ground when you can, but if you need a release, take comfort in quietly thinking to yourself, "I'm really glad I'm not you..." and leave it at that.

Don't ~ forget, though, that some people have emotional or physical things going on beneath the surface, and if we knew what they were, we'd cut them a lot more slack.

Don't ~ ever forget that reckless behavior and cars are a
  deadly mix. People forget that every year, and when they
  do, it's often the last thing they'll ever forget.
Don't ~ be afraid to ask for advice. There are people who love
  you and care about you and would love to help you in
  any way they can. Be brave... and ask.
Don't ~ be obsessive about your body and your looks. You're
  growing and changing and you are a work in progress and
  a miracle in the making. The simple truth in the looks
  department is — some people are always going to seem
  better and others will always seem worse. It's okay. We're
  all different. That's pretty much the way the world works.
Don't ~ stop there: it's the same with money. There are the
  have-nots, the have-a-lots, and everybody in between.
  When your perspective gets lost and you're fretting about
  not having something "everyone else" has, remember,
  some can't afford the cost of anything.
Don't ~ let cynical people transfer their cynicism off on you.
  In spite of all its problems, it is still a pretty amazing
  world and there are lots of truly wonderful people
  spinning around on this planet.
And don't ~ ever forget: the teen years can definitely be
  challenging, but if you work it right... they're also some
  of the most memorable and most fun and most
    amazing times of life.
                                    — Douglas Pagels

When I was a teenager, if someone had told me that one day I would look back and be grateful for [what] I was going through; that it would make me a better person when I grew up, I would have thought they were crazy. Now, as a mature woman, I can't believe this has actually happened....

I would not wish my early life on anyone, but it is my life. It's a large part of who I am now. The pain I went through as a teen strengthened me and taught me the truth of that wonderful adage about doing unto others as you would wish them to do unto you. I have discovered that doing what you love actually enhances your chances for success, and treating people as you want to be treated is a good way to make friends and do business.

— Jodee Blanco

I do wish you all the best.
Luck helps, and life gets easier
once you get the hang of it....

Take care of yourself.
You have a lot
to look forward to.

❖ Carol Weston

Social... Security

Some of the luckiest people in the world are those who have a wonderful friend to share life with...

A friend who cares and who shares the gifts of smiles and closeness and companionship. Someone with whom you have so much in common. Somebody who's a precious part of the best memories you'll ever make. A special friend. A true friend. One to confide in, one who never lets you down, and one who always understands. A friend who is simply amazing because their heart is so big, their soul is so beautiful, and because everything about them inspires everything that is good about you.

— Douglas Pagels

Not using good judgment in choosing your friends and hanging out with the wrong crowd can undermine all the good things you've done and great decisions you've made.

— Serena Williams

You don't need a certain number of friends, only a number of friends you can be certain of.

— Anonymous

Don't hang out with anyone who doesn't understand why you're so wonderful, or who needs to be told, or who doesn't tell you at regular intervals when you forget.

— Lisa Scottoline

A friend is one of the nicest
things you can have —
and one of the best
things you can be.

❖ Douglas Pagels

It took almost a year before I had a secure group of friends. It was hard going to school functions and games when I didn't know whether I'd have anyone to sit with. There were times when I sat alone. But I learned that if I smiled and tried to get to know everybody, most people smiled back. I can't help feeling that learning this did more than help make the move easier in high school. I think it will help me move into new and unfamiliar situations all through life.

— Natalie Fuller

You know how sometimes you feel incredibly self-conscious, like everyone's looking at you? The minute you smile, you're telling the world that you think you look terrific, and when you do that, the world's likely to believe you. You do something else with that smile: you take the focus off yourself and reach out to all those other kids who are also feeling self-conscious. By smiling, you say, "Hey, I like you." When you do that, you help build their confidence, and they're bound to like you for that.

Smile, and everybody wins.

— Joni Arredia

One of the most important parts of being a winner in life is being happy. A happy person makes those around them happy as well, and that is one of the greatest gifts of all. Make decisions in your life that lead to happiness.

— Mia Hamm

It doesn't matter if your eyes are brown or green, if you're tall or small, or what your skin color is. The outside is a shell that holds the real you: your essence, your spirit. In order to truly shine, you need to feel good on the inside....

You may not love every single one of your features (few people actually do), but if you work on viewing yourself as a complete person who has strengths, dreams, and goals, you'll begin to feel more comfortable with who you are. Your enthusiasm for life will radiate outward, and other people will notice....

When your inner qualities shine, people are drawn to you. They like who you are and how you make them feel.

— Tina Schwager, PTA, ATC and Michele Schuerger

Be Yourself

Hold on to your dreams, and never let them go ♦
Show the world how wonderful you are ♦ Wish on a
star that shines in your sky ♦ Rely on all the strength
you have inside ♦ Stay in touch with those who touch
your life with love ♦ Look on the bright side and don't
let adversity keep you from winning ♦ Be yourself,
because you are filled with special qualities that have
brought you this far and that will always see you
through ♦ Keep your spirits up ♦ Make your heart
happy, and let it reflect on everything you do!

— Douglas Pagels

May success and a smile always be yours, even when you are knee-deep in the sticky mud of life.

— Kermit the Frog

Some parts of life have to be messy before they can become beautiful.

— Natasha Bedingfield

It is normal for your self-esteem to drop once you have reached adolescence, but fortunately this is temporary if you deal with it in healthy ways. Don't put pressure on yourself to be perfect in every way. Just because you don't get straight A's doesn't mean that you are a slacker, and having a messy room doesn't make you a slob. Everyone has strengths, and the key to good self-esteem is recognizing your strong points and building on them. The sooner you do this, the sooner you will be on the road to a better, more positive self-image.

— Amanda Ford

Life is like a ten-speed bike. Most of us have gears we never use.

❖ Charles M. Schulz

If You Do These Ten Things...
you will be able to see your way through just about anything

♦ Stay positive! (Hopeful people are happier people.) ♦ Choose wisely. (Good choices will come back to bless you.) ♦ Remember what matters. (The present moment. The good people in it. Hopes and dreams and feelings.)

♦ Don't stress out over things you can't control. (Just don't.) ♦ Count every blessing. (Even the little ones add up to a lot.) ♦ Be good to your body. (It's the only one you get.)

♦ Listen to the wishes of your heart. (It always seems to know what's true, what's right, what to do, and where to go with your life.)

♦ Understand how special you are! ♦ Realize how strong you can be. ♦ And know that, YES, you're going to make it through, no matter what.

Maybe you won't be dancing in the streets or jumping on the bed... but you are going to get through the day, the night, and each and every moment that lies ahead. (I promise.)

— Douglas Pagels

I was not the brightest star in my class by far. I was always in a bit of trouble, nothing interesting. But my presence here today is a testament to all late bloomers.
— Sigourney Weaver

I sometimes feel like a late bloomer. I feel it would have been possible to do much more, much sooner, if I hadn't been so worried. What I know now... is that there's no time to waste. It's time to be bold about who you really are.
— Ann Curry

I believe that you tend to create your own blessings. You have to prepare yourself so that when opportunity comes, you're ready.
— Oprah Winfrey

Things That Are Going to Happen in Your Life... (if they haven't already)

- You will be concerned about your future, wonder what's to come, and be uncertain how you'll manage.

- You will manage. As a matter of fact, you'll succeed.

- You will have friendships you will treasure forever.

- You will experience life's immense joys and deep sorrows.

- You will make memories you wouldn't trade for anything.

- You will have times you'd just as soon forget.

- You will be in difficult situations, in places you'd rather not be, or with others who jeopardize your well-being.

- You will come out of it just fine, as long as you do whatever it takes to get yourself into a better place and put control of the situation into your own hands, not at the whim of someone else.

- You will eventually, proudly, happily discover that all the good things you can do — having the right attitude, having a strong belief in your abilities, making good choices and responsible decisions — all those good things you can do will pay huge dividends.

- You'll see. Your prayers will be heard.

- Your karma will kick in.

- The sacrifices you made will be repaid.

- And the good work will have all been worth it.

— Douglas Pagels

If I had just one wish,
I'd visit younger days.
And tell the younger me,
"It all works out okay."

❖ Jessica Somers

I Wish for You

Happiness. Deep down within.
Serenity. With each sunrise.
Success. In each facet of your life.
Close and caring friends.
Love. That never ends.

Special memories. Of all
    the yesterdays.
A bright today. With so much
    to be thankful for.
A path. That leads to
    beautiful tomorrows.

Dreams. That do their best to come true.
And appreciation. Of all the wonderful
        things about you.

— Douglas Pagels

Acknowledgments

We gratefully acknowledge the permission granted by the following authors, publishers, and authors' representatives to reprint poems or excerpts from their publications.

Tiger Beat for "We're growing and we're going…" by Selena Gomez from "Awww… Selena Gomez Says Justin Bieber Is Protective over Her" (*Tiger Beat*: April 13, 2010). Copyright © 2010 by Laufer Media, Inc. All rights reserved.

Flare for "I am in a transitional period…" by Emma Watson from "Harry Potter's Emma Watson (Like You've Never Seen Her Before)" by the Editors of *Flare* (Flare.com: November 2008). Copyright © 2008 by *Flare*. All rights reserved.

Joni Arredia for "It is wonderful to be a…," "Dreams are your destination…," and "You know how sometimes…" from SEX, BOYS & YOU. Copyright © 1998 by Joni Arredia. All rights reserved.

HarperCollins Publishers for "Just remember from one…" by Niki Taylor, "My message to teens…" by Brooke Shields, "Being a teenager is hard…" by Phoebe Cates, and "I don't need to tell you…" by Bobbi Brown from TEENAGE BEAUTY by Bobbi Brown. Copyright © 2000 by Bobbi Brown Book, LLC, and Annemarie Iverson. All rights reserved. And for "My daily mission…" from IT'S NOT ABOUT THE BRA by Brandi Chastain. Copyright © 2004 by Brandi Chastain. All rights reserved. And for "I think actress Kate Winslet…" and "While body type is something…" from TEENAGE FITNESS: GET FIT, LOOK GOOD, AND FEEL GREAT! by Kathy Kaehler. Copyright © 2001 by Kathy Kaehler. All rights reserved. And for "I was an eighteen-year-old kid…" from CHASING DOWN THE DAWN by Jewel Kilcher. Copyright © 2000 by Jewel Kilcher. All rights reserved. And for "I have lost a lot of friends…" from LADIES FIRST by Queen Latifah and Karen Hunter. Copyright © 1999 by Queen Latifah, Inc. All rights reserved. And for "One of the most important parts…" from GO FOR THE GOAL by Mia Hamm and Aaron Heifetz. Copyright © 1999 by Mia Hamm. All rights reserved.

Carol Weston, www.carolweston.com, for "One of the great things…," "School exposes you to so much…," "I'm hoping you don't smoke…," and "I do wish you all the best" from GIRLTALK, FOURTH EDITION. Copyright © 2004 by Carol Weston. All rights reserved.

Da Capo Press, a Member of the Perseus Books Group, for "Know that you are loved…" by Mýa Harrison, "It's your choice" by Sara Blakely, "You have everything you need inside…" by Aimee Mullins, "I want you to know that your…" by Magali Amadei, "If I could say anything…" by Jessica Alba, and "Some parts of life…" by Natasha Bedingfield from IF I'D KNOWN THEN: WOMEN IN THEIR 20s WRITE LETTERS TO THEIR YOUNGER SELVES, edited by Ellyn Spragins. Copyright © 2008 by Ellyn Spragins. All rights reserved. And for "Do I love my body?" from LOCKER ROOM DIARIES by Leslie Goldman. Copyright © 2006 by Leslie Goldman. All rights reserved.

Cader Books for "You are capable of more…" by Edward O. Wilson from THE MOST IMPORTANT THINGS I KNOW, compiled by Lorne A. Adrain. Copyright © 1997 by Lorne A. Adrain. All rights reserved.

Scholastic, Inc., for "Give from your heart…" from GIRLS HOLD UP THIS WORLD by Jada Pinkett Smith. Copyright © 2005 by Jada Pinkett Smith. All rights reserved.

Barbour Publishing, Inc., for "Make each day, each stage…" by Faith Stewart from GOOD JOB! I'M PROUD OF YOU, written and compiled by Ellyn Sanna. Copyright © 2000 by Barbour Publishing, Inc. All rights reserved.

Broadway Books, a division of Random House, Inc., for "I've got something to say…" by Trisha Yearwood, "Don't hang out with anyone who…" by Lisa Scottoline, and "I sometimes feel like…" by Ann Curry from WHAT I KNOW NOW, edited by Ellyn Spragins. Copyright © 2006 by Ellyn Spragins. All rights reserved.

G.P. Putnam's Sons, a division of Penguin Group (USA), Inc., for "This was the turning point for me…" and "People… can constantly put…" from TEARS FOR WATER: SONGBOOK OF POEMS AND LYRICS by Alicia Keys. Copyright © 2004 by Lellow Brands, Inc. All rights reserved.

Gotham Books, an imprint of Penguin Group (USA), Inc., for "Whatever your goal…" from "Prologue" by Annika Sorenstam and "To be the best at anything…" from "Foreword" by Celine Dion from GOLF ANNIKA'S WAY by Annika Sorenstam, with the editors of *Golf* magazine. Copyright © 2004 by Esch & Stam, Inc. All rights reserved.

Telegraph Media Group Limited for "Basically, all the record companies…" by Taylor Swift from "Taylor Swift: the 19 year old country music star conquering America — and now Britain" by John Preston (*Telegraph*: April 26, 2009). Copyright © 2009 by Telegraph Media Group Limited. All rights reserved.

International Youth Foundation for "Learn to make a way out of no way" by Marian Wright Edelman from OUR TIME IS NOW: YOUNG PEOPLE CHANGING THE WORLD, edited by Sheila Kinkade and Christina Macy. Copyright © 2005 by International Youth Foundation. All rights reserved.

Paulist Press, Inc., www.paulistpress.com, for "How does one become a butterfly?" from HOPE FOR THE FLOWERS by Trina Paulus. Copyright © 1997 by Trina Paulus. All rights reserved.

Crown Publishers, a division of Random House, Inc. for "I want you to enjoy your life…" by Joyce A. Ladner, "Once you know what is right and wrong…" and "Do the Right Thing!" by Rebecca Lobo, and "I was not the brightest star…" by Sigourney Weaver from 33 THINGS EVERY GIRL SHOULD KNOW, edited by Tonya Bolden. Copyright © 1998 by Tonya Bolden. All rights reserved.

Faith Words, a division of Hachette Book Group, for "I believe that all of us…" from ENJOYING WHERE YOU ARE ON THE WAY TO WHERE YOU ARE GOING by Joyce Meyer. Copyright © 1996 by Joyce Meyer. Reprinted by permission of Faith Words. All rights reserved.

John Wiley & Sons, Inc., for "Whatever good you put out…" and "I believe that you tend…" by Oprah Winfrey from OPRAH WINFREY SPEAKS by Janet Lowe. Copyright © 1998 by Janet Lowe. Reprinted by permission. All rights reserved.

Abrams, www.hnabooks.com, for "I'm still in the process…" by Lucy Smith from SEEN AND HEARD, edited by Mary Motley Kalegris. Copyright © 1998 by Mary Motley Kalegris. All rights reserved.

J. Countryman, a division of Thomas Nelson, Inc., Nashville, Tennessee, for "In junior high…" from GENUINE: BEING REAL IN AN ARTIFICIAL WORLD by Stacie Orrico. Copyright © 2001 by Stacie Orrico. All rights reserved.